CA

HAYLEY
WICKENHEISER

BY TODD KORTEMEIER

PRESS BOX
BOOKS

Press Box Books is an imprint of Press Room Editions.

This book is distributed exclusively in Canada by Saunders Book Company, PO Box 308, Collingwood ON L9Y 3Z7. For sales information, call 800-461-9120, or email info@saundersbook.ca. **www.saundersbook.ca**

Produced for Press Box Books by Red Line Editorial.

Photographs ©: Mark Humphrey/AP Images, cover, 1; Carl Sandin/Bildbyran/Icon Sportswire, 4; Michael Kappeler/DPA/ZumaPress/Icon Sportswire, 6; Wa Funches/AP Images, 9; Frank Gunn/The Canadian Press/AP Images, 13; Rick Stewart/Allspo/Getty Images, 15; Lutz Bongartz/Bongarts/Getty Images, 16; George Widman/AP Images, 19; NIKO/DPPI-SIPA/Icon Sportswire, 20; Toronto Star/ZumaPress/Icon Sportswire, 22; Gene J. Puskar/AP Images, 24, 30; Paul Chiasson/The Canadian Press/AP Images, 26; Red Line Editorial/bergserg/Shutterstock Images, 29

ISBN
978-1-62143-2906 (hardcover)
978-1-62143-2999 (paperback)
978-1-62143-3088 (hosted ebook)

Library of Congress Control Number: 2015939660

Printed in the United States of America
Mankato, MN
July, 2015

CONTENTS

CHAPTER 1
CARRYING THE MAPLE LEAF — 5

CHAPTER 2
PLAYING WITH THE BOYS — 8

CHAPTER 3
GROWING WITH THE SPORT — 14

CHAPTER 4
BEST OF THE BEST — 18

CHAPTER 5
NEVER SLOWING DOWN — 23

Timeline Map — 28
Hayley Wickenheiser at a Glance — 30
Glossary — 31
For More Information — 31
Index — 32
About the Author — 32

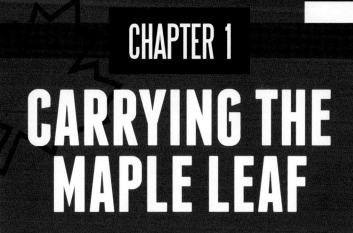

CHAPTER 1
CARRYING THE MAPLE LEAF

A pack of athletes dressed in red appeared at Fisht Olympic Stadium in Sochi, Russia. It was the Canadian Olympic team. And at the front of the group, waving a giant Canadian flag, was hockey star Hayley Wickenheiser. She was Team Canada's flag bearer at the 2014 Olympic Winter Games.

Canada had many great athletes at the Olympics. Those athletes picked

Hayley Wickenheiser leads Team Canada into the 2014 Olympics opening ceremony.

Wickenheiser to carry the flag. She was certainly deserving. Wickenheiser had played with the national team for 20 years. She had won three Olympic gold medals and one silver. Plus, she had won the Women's World Championship seven times.

Three billion people watched the opening ceremony. Flag bearers always receive a lot of attention. That attention can be distracting. Some previous flag bearers even said the distraction had affected their performance. But Wickenheiser was not bothered by the attention. She knew it was a great honour. And she felt the support of her country and teammates.

Wickenheiser already felt pressure to succeed. She played hockey for Canada. Expectations were always high. Carrying a flag was nothing compared to that. The only thing she was concerned about was embarrassing herself by tripping.

Softball Star

Wickenheiser also was a great softball player. She was a stellar shortstop and hitter. Softball was part of the Olympics from 1996–2008. Wickenheiser made Canada's Olympic softball team in 2000. She had debuted in the Winter Games two years earlier. Only one Canadian woman had previously competed in both the Summer and Winter Games. However, Wickenheiser was the first to do it in two team sports.

As Wickenheiser led Canada into the stadium, she had time to enjoy the moment. But she did not have long. Soon, she would need to turn her attention back to the ice. She and Canada had their first game the next day. A fourth Olympic gold medal was on the line.

CHAPTER 2
PLAYING WITH THE BOYS

Few girls played hockey when Hayley Marie Wickenheiser was born on August 12, 1978. That was especially true in her hometown of Shaunavon, Saskatchewan. It was very small. Many boys played hockey there. But girls didn't have the same opportunities.

That didn't stop Hayley. She was determined to play. Her parents were both teachers who worked with the local rink. They often brought Hayley along. One day, when she was around three years old, she got tired of watching. She asked her parents if she could play. They said yes.

Hayley loved the game. Her dad built a rink in their backyard. On that rink she learned and perfected her famous slap shot. When not playing, the family loved watching the Edmonton Oilers. No National Hockey League (NHL) team was better in the 1980s. Hayley and her dad watched such stars as Wayne Gretzky and Mark Messier.

Hometown Hero

Hayley's hometown gave her a special honour in 2006. The sportsplex in Shaunavon was renamed Wickenheiser Place. In 2011, a new arena was built. It's called the Crescent Point Wickenheiser Centre. Hayley cut the ribbon to open the building. There also is a sign in town saying "Home of Hayley Wickenheiser." It was put up in 2001.

Growing up, all Hayley knew was boys' and men's hockey. Women didn't yet play in the Olympics. The first Women's World Championship was not held until 1990. In fact, for a long time she didn't even know other girls who played hockey.

When she was eight, Hayley wanted to attend a hockey school. She was told it was for boys only. But Hayley's mother didn't accept that. She convinced the school to accept Hayley. Hayley soon became the first girl player in its history.

Boys' teams allowed Hayley to play. But boys' hockey could be hard. Some of the boys didn't think a girl should play with them. Even some parents felt that way. This made Hayley feel left out. She sometimes avoided her teammates. She'd hide until it was time to hit the ice. The experience was challenging. But it only made Hayley work harder. She wanted to show everybody she belonged.

Everything changed for Hayley in 1990. She was 12 years old when the first Women's World Championship was held that year in Ottawa. Team Canada beat Team USA for the win. Watching the great women's players on TV inspired Hayley. She wanted to play at that level, too.

QUICK STAT

Hayley had six points (three goals, three assists) in six games at the Canada Winter Games.

She took a major step toward that goal that year. The family moved to Calgary. An all-girls team called Team Alberta was based there. Finally, Hayley could play with other girls. It didn't even matter that her teammates were much older.

Team Alberta played in the 1991 Canada Winter Games. The tournament was for girls as old as 18.

Yet 12-year-old Hayley was the star. She scored the tournament-winning goal. Soon after, she was named the tournament's Most Valuable Player (MVP).

Hayley only got better. She continued playing mostly with boys. And by the time she was 15, she was one of the best players her age in Calgary. That included both boys and girls. By then, women's hockey had begun to grow. Many countries had women's national teams. And in 1994, Team Canada called Hayley for the first time. At 15 she was the youngest player on the team. Yet she helped Canada win at the World Championship. It was the beginning of a long career with Team Canada.

CHAPTER 3
GROWING WITH THE SPORT

Wickenheiser had been a star at all levels. The 1994 Women's World Championship introduced her to more fans. They saw she could be a special player at the top level, too. But Wickenheiser knew she would have to work hard to become the best.

When playing with Team Canada, she worked closely with the older players. Wickenheiser watched how they prepared for games. She watched how they battled hard all game long. Those players taught Wickenheiser about winning and leadership.

Team Canada only played a handful of games each year. The rest of the time Wickenheiser stayed in Alberta. Preparation was key to Wickenheiser's success. She used to spend hours on her backyard rink. She practiced her skills over and over. Soon, she no longer had to think about her skills. She could just do them.

Wickenheiser, *left*, battles for the puck with a Team USA player during the 1998 Olympics.

This preparation helped Wickenheiser get better. It also helped her become a leader. Teammates noticed she always prepared the same way. Her example made them want to work harder, too.

Team Canada won the World Championship again in 1997. The big test came one year later. The World Championship had shown that women could play great hockey. So women's hockey was added to the Olympic Winter Games for 1998 in Nagano, Japan.

Wickenheiser was just 19 years old. Yet she was already a star. She opened the Olympics with a goal and two assists in the first game. Canada beat Japan 13–0. Both Team Canada and Team USA started 4–0. The rivals were assured of meeting in the gold-medal game. But first, they met in the final opening-round game.

Becoming a Mom

In 2000 Wickenheiser became a mom. She adopted a son named Noah. He was still a baby. Noah grew up not liking hockey. He didn't like how busy it kept his mom. But he's been by her side for many of her biggest moments. He's been on the ice after gold-medal games.

The Canada players were confident. Canada had won all four World Championship tournaments. But Team USA finished second every time. And in this game, Team USA shocked Canada with a 7–4 win. Then, in the gold-medal game, Team USA did so again, winning 3–1. Wickenheiser and her teammates left Japan with silver medals.

Wickenheiser skates against Sweden during the 2006 Olympic gold-medal game.

Soon after, Wickenheiser got a tryout with a men's professional team in Finland. This time she made the team, HC Salamat. On February 1, 2003, Wickenheiser scored her first goal. No woman had ever scored in a professional men's league. However, Wickenheiser left Finland in the 2003–04 season. She wasn't playing as much as she wanted.

Instead she joined a new women's league in Canada in 2004–05. The league had many of the world's best players. It proved to be a good fit. Wickenheiser was the league's MVP. Plus, her team won the league championship.

The 2006 Olympics were in Turin, Italy. At 27, Wickenheiser was in her prime. That showed throughout the tournament. Team Canada won its first four games. Wickenheiser scored in all four. Her performance sent Canada back to the gold-medal game. This time Canada faced Sweden. Wickenheiser had two assists in the game. Canada won 4–1. In total, Wickenheiser had five goals and 12 assists. Once again she was named Olympics MVP. And once again, there was little doubt that she was the world's best player.

Giving Back

Wickenheiser knows that she can use her fame to help others. One charity she works with is called Right to Play. It brings sports and healthy activities to poorer countries around the world. Wickenheiser has travelled to Africa with Right to Play. She also visits schools and speaks to children about being healthy and active.

CHAPTER 5

NEVER SLOWING DOWN

Female hockey players don't make much money. Many leave the sport in their mid-20s to find other jobs. Wickenheiser was 27 in 2006. She had already won two Olympic gold medals. But she wasn't ready to stop. The 2010 Olympics would be in Vancouver. Wickenheiser and her Canada teammates wanted to win another gold medal on home ice.

Wickenheiser unleashes a shot against Switzerland at the 2010 Olympics.

Wickenheiser races up the ice against Sweden in the 2010 Olympics.

Wickenheiser joined a Swedish men's team called Eskilstuna Linden in 2008–09. The players were big and strong. They also were allowed to check. Wickenheiser was not afraid of the rough play. She used the experience to become a better player.

Her focus turned back to Team Canada after that. Excitement for the Olympics was growing in Canada. But the players had to stay focused. Team USA had won the Women's World Championship in 2008 and 2009. Meanwhile, Wickenheiser was now 31 years old. She wasn't as fast as she used to be. But she had experience. She knew how to prepare for big games. And before the Games, she was named team captain. She would officially be Team Canada's leader.

Team Canada started fast at the Olympics. It swept the first three games. Canada scored 41 goals and gave up just two. Wickenheiser had two goals and nine assists in those games. In addition, she was an amazing plus-14.

Olympic Oath

The Olympic oath is a great tradition. One athlete is chosen to read the oath at each opening ceremony. In 2010 Wickenheiser was that athlete. The oath is a promise to follow the Olympic ideals. The athletes promise to compete fairly and with good sportsmanship.

Team Canada then shut out Finland 5–0 in the semi-finals. That set up a big gold-medal game. Team USA had also gone undefeated. Fans packed the arena. Even Prime Minister Stephen Harper was at the game. He wore Wickenheiser's jersey. She did not score in the game. But Canada battled all game to win 2–0. The victory set off a huge celebration. The Canada players stayed on the ice for a long time after the game.

Some believed Wickenheiser might retire after that. She had accomplished more than any other women's player. But she still had the drive to keep playing. She joined the University of Calgary Dinos. There she could play hockey and be a full-time student. Her goal is to become a doctor after her hockey days.

Her hockey days weren't close to being over, though. Wickenheiser graduated in 2013. Then she turned her attention back to Team Canada. Wickenheiser was 35. Only one teammate was older. Yet the 2014 Olympics in Sochi, Russia, was more of the same. Wickenheiser had two goals and three assists in five games. Canada again won the gold medal. And afterward, Wickenheiser said she hoped to compete in the next Olympics in 2018.

Video Game Star

Until 2012, hockey video games never featured women. Wickenheiser was the first. She and Team USA defenceman Angela Ruggiero were included in *NHL 13*.

Timeline Map

1. **Shaunavon, Saskatchewan 1978**
   Hayley Marie Wickenheiser is born on August 12. She
   lives in Shaunavon until age 12.

2. **Charlottetown, Prince Edward Island 1991**
   As a 12-year-old, Wickenheiser leads Team Alberta to
   victory at the Canada Winter Games. She is the MVP of
   the tournament for players 18-and-under.

3. **Lake Placid, New York 1994**
   Wickenheiser joins Team Canada at the Women's World
   Championships for the first time. Canada beats Team USA
   to win the title.

4. **Philadelphia, Pennsylvania 1998**
   Wickenheiser participates in a rookie training camp
   with other players trying to make the NHL's Philadelphia
   Flyers. She tries out again in 1999.

5. **Salt Lake City, Utah 2002**
   Wickenheiser leads Team Canada to its first Olympic gold
   medal. She is named tournament MVP. She is Olympics
   MVP in 2006 as Canada wins again in Turin, Italy.

6. **Vancouver, British Columbia 2010**
   Competing on home ice, Wickenheiser and Team Canada
   beat Team USA to claim the Olympic gold medal.

7. **Calgary, Alberta 2010–13**
   Wickenheiser attends and plays hockey at the University
   of Calgary.

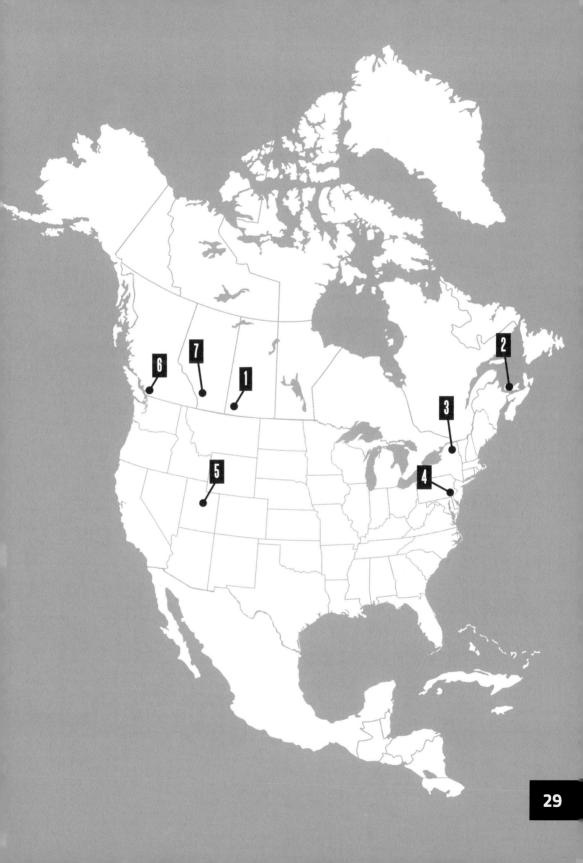

Hayley Wickenheiser at a Glance

FULL NAME: Hayley Marie Wickenheiser

BIRTH DATE: August 12, 1978

BIRTHPLACE: Shaunavon, Saskatchewan

TEAM CANADA:

- Olympic Games: 1998 (second place), 2002 (first), 2006 (first), 2010 (first), 2014 (first)
- Women's World Championship: 1994 (first), 1997 (first), 1999 (first), 2000 (first), 2004 (first), 2005 (second), 2007 (first), 2008 (second), 2009 (second), 2011 (second), 2012 (first), 2013 (second)
- Honours: Olympics MVP 2002, 2006; Olympic team captain 2010; Team Canada flag bearer 2014

OTHER HONOURS:

- Competed for Team Canada in softball at the 2000 Olympics
- Participated in the Philadelphia Flyers' rookie camp in 1998, 1999
- Became first woman to record a point in a men's professional game

BEST OLYMPIC PERFORMANCES:

GOALS	ASSISTS	POINTS
7 (2002)	12 (2006)	17 (2006)

Glossary

CAPTAIN: the on-ice leader of a hockey team

CHARITY: an organization founded to help other people

OATH: a promise

POINT: a goal or an assist

POWER PLAY: when one team has a one- or two-player advantage on the ice due to a penalty or penalties by the other team

REBOUND: a loose puck in front of the goal, immediately after a shot

For More Information

BOOKS

Borth, Teddy. *Hockey: Great Moments, Records, and Facts.* Minneapolis, MN: Abdo Publishing, 2015.

Peters, Chris. *Great Moments in Olympic Ice Hockey.* Minneapolis, MN: Abdo Publishing, 2015.

WEB SITES

Hayley Wickenheiser
www.hayleywickenheiser.com

Hockey Canada
www.hockeycanada.ca

Index

Canada Olympic Team. *See* Team Canada

Canada Winter Games, 11–12

Crescent Point Wickenheiser Centre, 10

Edmonton Oilers, 9

Eskilstuna Linden, 24

family, 8–9, 10, 17

Gretzky, Wayne, 9

Harper, Steven, 26

HC Salamat, 20

Messier, Mark, 9

NHL 13, 27

Olympics, 5–7, 10, 16–17, 18–19, 21, 23, 25–26, 27

Philadelphia Flyers, 18

Right to Play, 21

Ruggiero, Angela, 27

Shaunavon, Saskatchewan, 8, 10

softball, 7

Team Alberta, 11–12

Team Canada, 5, 7, 11, 12, 14–15, 16–17, 18–19, 21, 23, 25–26, 27

University of Calgary, 27

Wickenheiser, Noah (son), 17

Wickenheiser Place, 10

Women's World Championship, 6, 10, 11, 12, 14, 16, 17, 18, 25

About the Author

Todd Kortemeier is a writer and journalist from Minneapolis. He is a graduate of the University of Minnesota's School of Journalism & Mass Communication.